Fun Ways to Learn the Whole Story of Jesus and His Love

Jesus Grows Up

Creative Bible-Learning Activities for Children Ages 6-12

Copyright © 1991 by Tracy Leffingwell Harrast. Published by David C. Cook Publishing Co.
Printed in the United States of America.

All puzzles and Bible activities are based on the NIV.

Scripture taken from the Holy Bible, New International Version, Copyright © 1973,
1978, 1984 International Bible Society.
Used by permission of Zondervan Bible Publishers.

Book Design by Tabb Associates
Cover Illustration by Gary Locke
Interior Illustrations by Anne Kennedy

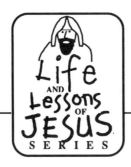

To My Children and Others Who Read This Book

The Bible doesn't tell us very much about what Jesus was like as a boy, but we do know Jesus was the only person who never did anything wrong (see Hebrews 4:15). Even though we try to be like Him, we all make mistakes, but we can be forgiven because Jesus died for us.

Pray for the Lord to make you how He wants you to be, and you'll become more like Jesus every day.

—Tracy L. Harrast

Jesus Grows Up

CONTENTS

Palestine, Where Jesus Grew Up

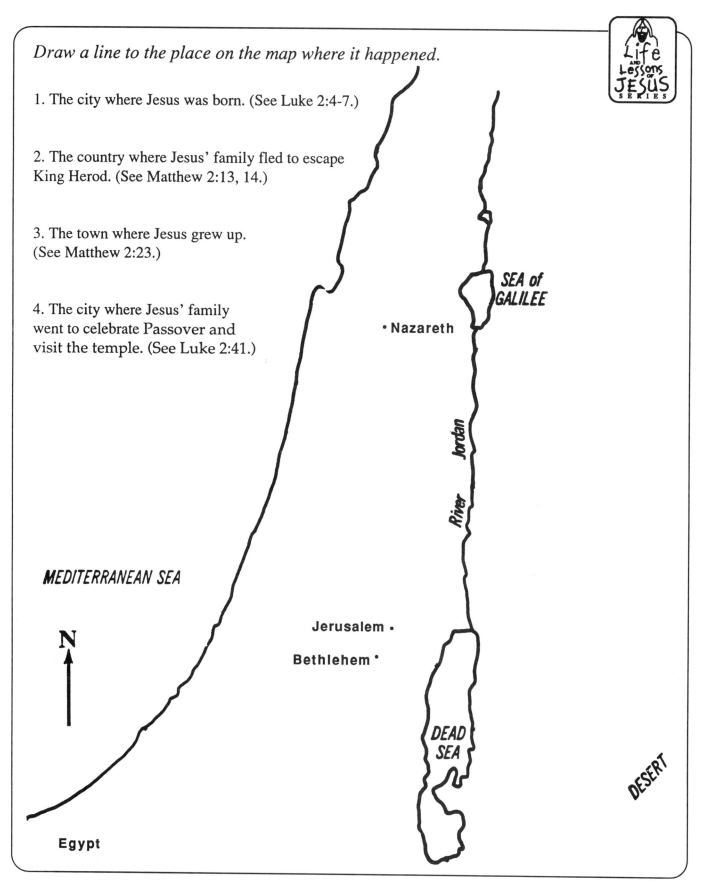

Draw a line to the place on the map where it happened.

1. The city where Jesus was born. (See Luke 2:4-7.)

2. The country where Jesus' family fled to escape King Herod. (See Matthew 2:13, 14.)

3. The town where Jesus grew up. (See Matthew 2:23.)

4. The city where Jesus' family went to celebrate Passover and visit the temple. (See Luke 2:41.)

SEA of GALILEE

• Nazareth

River Jordan

MEDITERRANEAN SEA

N

Jerusalem •

Bethlehem •

DEAD SEA

DESERT

Egypt

Life AND Lessons OF JESUS SERIES

What's That?

How well do you know the story of Jesus' birth? Read about it in Luke 2:1-7 in the King James Bible. Then, draw a line from each word to what it means. Then draw a line from the meaning to the picture it matches.

Swaddling

1. A place where animal feed was kept. In Bible times, it was usually carved in a wall.

Manger

2. A place where animals were kept. In those days, some were caves.

Stable

3. Clothes for wrapping a baby.

Inn

4. Money that was paid to the leaders of the country.

Tax

5. A place for people to stay when they traveled.

Draw a star in this box when you've read Luke 2:1-7.

6

When Was Jesus Born?

HEROD DIED ——————→

8 7 6 5 4 3 3 2 1 • 1(A.D.) 2 3 4 5 6 7 8

THE CREATION ◁ B.C.(BEFORE CHRIST) ▷ A.D. (ANNO DOMINI) ▷ NOW

Almost 600 years after Jesus was born, the calendar was changed so that years would be counted by whether they were before or after the birth of Jesus. The years before Jesus was born were labeled B.C. (Before Christ). The years were counted backward from the time Christ was born. For example, the year 5 B.C. came before the year 4 B.C. The years after Jesus was born were called A.D. (*Anno Domini,* which means "in the year of our Lord").

Use the facts below to figure out when Jesus might have been born.

FACT: Matthew 2:1 says Jesus was born while Herod was king.
FACT: Herod died in the year 4 B.C.
FACT: Matthew 2:16 shows that Jesus may have been at least two years old when Herod died.

1. What is definitely the latest date that Jesus could have been born? (Hint: the year Herod died) _____
2. What year is likely the earliest year Jesus could have been born? (Hint: two years before Herod died) _____
3. How many years has it probably been since Jesus was born? (Hint: add your answer from question #2 to the current year) _____

If you made a birthday cake for Jesus this year, how many candles should it probably have? (Your answer from question #3.)

Write that number on the cake.

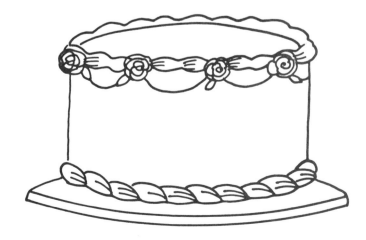

What a Little Bird Tells Us About Joseph and Mary

Read these words and pictures to discover an interesting fact about Jesus' parents, Mary and Joseph.

W+ 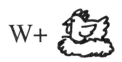 were   b +  - c,   + ents

h + - m   2   t +  - c   A and   A

   2   the   .   If   th + A   were

temple

p + - d,   th + A   could   b +    2   .

It   is   1 + - b + ly   t +   and were

Joseph   Mary

p + - d   + cause   th + A   brought   A

2nd and   A .

Find Out What Simeon Said

When you play "Simon Says," you do only what Simon says, not what he doesn't say. In this game, you'll do what *Simeon* says, not what Simeon doesn't say. Simeon saw Jesus at the temple and said this about Him.

Simeon says, "Change every A to O and every O to A."
Change every B to Z and every Z to B.
Change every Y to R and every R to Y.
Simeon says, "Change every I to E and every E to I."
Simeon says, "Change every S to M and every M to S."

Thi Haly Mperet hod tald o son nosid Mesian thot hi wauld nat dei

_____

untel hi mow thi pirman wha wauld movi thi warld. Whin hi mow

_____

thi boby Jimum, Mesian moed, "Naw, E con dei en pioci." Hi kniw

_____

Jimum wom thi ane wha wauld movi thi warld. O wason nosid

_____

Onno kniw et, taa. Da yau knaw et?

_____

Draw a star in this box when you've read the story in Luke 2:25-35.

Jesus Escapes to Egypt

Someone was trying to kill the young Jesus! Read about His escape to Egypt. *Use the code to help you translate the story from "hieroglypics" (Egyptian picture writing) into English.*

Code:
angel = ○   Egypt = ↔   dream = 🐟   king = 🍁
Jesus = ♨   Joseph = 🦅   Mary = ☼   throne = 🦌

An ○ _____ appeared to 🦅 _____ in a 🐟 _____ and told him to take ☼ _____ and ♨ _____ to ↔ _____ and to stay there until the ○ _____ told him to bring them back. The ○ _____ said the cruel 🍁 _____ would try to kill ♨ _____. 🦅 _____ obeyed.

Herod was probably afraid that ♨ _____ would grow up and take his place on the 🦌 _____. After 🍁 _____ Herod died, 🦅 _____, ☼ _____, and ♨ _____ moved to Nazareth in Galilee.

Draw a star in this box when you've read the story in Matthew 2:13-23.

Make a Pyramid

Joseph obeyed God and took his family to Egypt. God wanted to protect Jesus. God's commands are always what will help us. Like Joseph, we can trust God's plans for us and obey Him. This week, after you pray and read your Bible, think of things God wants you to do and write them on the outside of your pyramid. When you've obeyed God, color that particular side of the pyramid.

What You Need
- typing paper
- pencil
- scissors
- tape

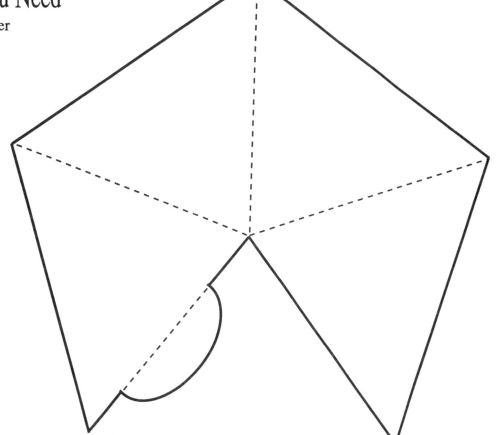

What You Do
1. Trace the pyramid pattern on this page onto the piece of typing paper.
2. In your own words, write the things you can do to obey and follow God this week.
3. Cut out your pyramid. Fold it along the dotted lines so plans to obey God are on the outside of the pyramid. Tuck in the tab, and tape it.

Clothes in Jesus' Day

Have you ever wondered what kind of clothes people in Bible times wore? They obviously didn't wear jeans and T-shirts. Jesus probably wore clothes like these when He was a boy.

The TUNIC was a short- or long-sleeved piece of clothing that came down to the knees or ankles. Poor people wore tunics made of goat's or camel's hair. This was rough material. Wealthy people wore tunics made of wool or linen, colored with expensive dyes.

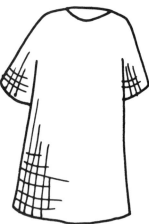

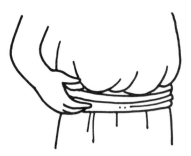

Instead of carrying a wallet, people pulled up their tunics to make a pouch above their belts where they carried valuables. This was called the BOSOM.

Some people, usually the poor, had CLOAKS that were more like a blanket than a coat. People wore them mostly in cool weather, and sometimes they covered their heads with them. At night they could wrap themselves in their cloaks to keep warm. People who had more money wore cloaks that were more like simple coats.

The belt was sometimes called the GIRDLE. When people needed to run or move freely, they pulled their tunics up through their girdles to leave their legs uncovered. This was called "girding up your loins."

Underwear was similar to shorts and was made of linen or leather. It was called a WAISTCLOTH.

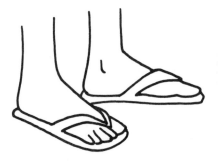

SANDALS were made of leather and had a flat sole. Two straps ran across the top of the foot and between the toes.

What Jesus Probably Wore

Write the name of each article of clothing in the blank next to it.

1._____

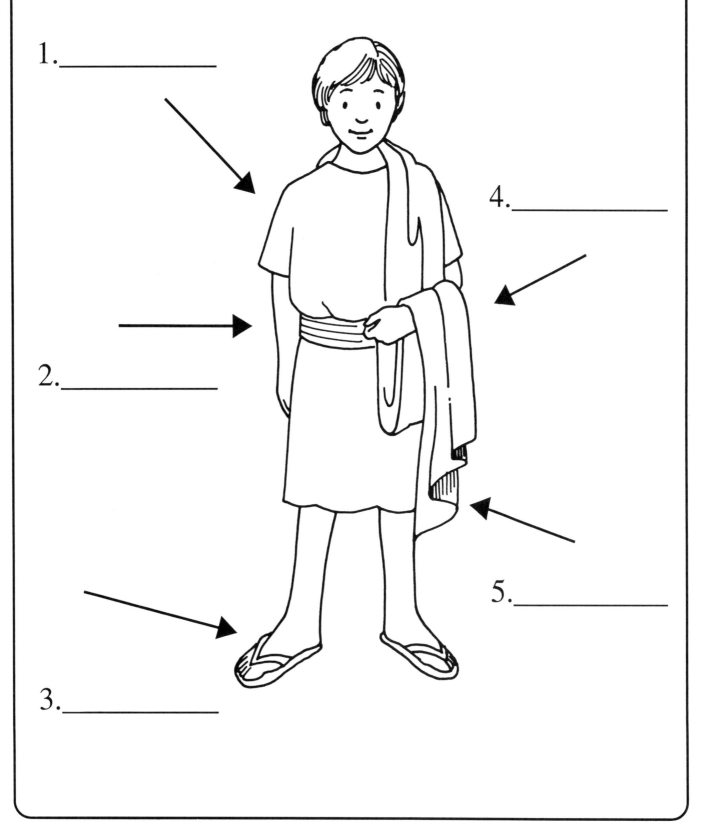

4._____

2._____

5._____

3._____

The Languages Jesus Spoke

ARAMAIC   GREEK   HEBREW

Jesus probably spoke at least three languages. He likely spoke *Aramaic* at home and with His friends. He spoke *Hebrew* when studying the Scriptures in the synagogue (Jewish church) and at school. He probably spoke Greek as well.

You may know and use some Hebrew words. Two Hebrew words are often used in worship. One means "praise the Lord." You might use this word in a worship song or psalm. Do you know what it is?
Unscramble these letters to discover the Hebrew word.
JLLAHAUELH

1. _____

Another word means "so let it be." You usually say this word at the end of your prayers. Do you know what it is?
Unscramble these letters to discover the Hebrew word. MAEN

2. _____

The Greek Alphabet

Here are the letters of the Greek alphabet. Try pronouncing the letters.

A	ălphă	H	ētă	N	nū	T	tău
B	bētă	Θ	thētă	Ξ	xī	Υ	ūpsilŏn
Γ	gămmă	I	īŏtă	O	omĭcrŏn	Φ	phī
Δ	dĕltă	K	kāppă	Π	pī	X	chī
E	ĕpsilŏn	Λ	lāmbdă	P	rhō	Ψ	psī
Z	zētă	M	mū	Σ	sĭgmă	Ω	ōmēgă

The Fish of Faith

After Jesus died, Christians were treated badly for their belief in Him. Many were put in prison or killed. Early Christians began using a symbol to let other Christians know secretly that they, too, believed in Jesus. The symbol looked like this:

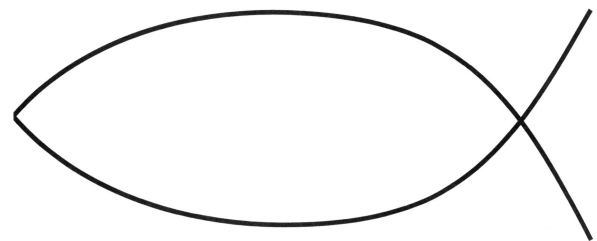

The Greek letters *iota, chi, theta, upsilon, and sigma* spell the word *fish* in Greek and were written inside the fish symbol. *Write those letters in the fish symbol above using the Greek alphabet on page 14*. Each letter stood for a Greek word. The words were *Jesus Christ, God's Son, Savior.*

Use the Greek letters on page 14 to write out the words below. Notice that the first letter of each word is found in the fish symbol above.

Jesus (iota eta sigma omicron upsilon sigma)

_____

Christ (chi rho iota sigma tau omicron sigma)

_____

God's (theta epsilon omicron upsilon)

_____

Son (upsilon iota omicron sigma)

_____

Savior (sigma omega tau eta rho)

_____

Money in Bible Times

The most common coin in Jesus' day was a denarius. This was a day's pay for a farm worker as well as a soldier. We don't know how much a denarius was worth.

Pretend that a worker today would earn $20.00 a day. That means that a denarius today would be worth $20.00. *Compare each coin with the denarius to figure out how much it might be worth today. Write the amount on each coin.*

Denarius

Day's pay for an average worker

Aureus

Worth 25 denarii
(25 x $20)

Didrachmon

Worth 1 1/2 denarii
(1 1/2 x $20)

Assarion

About 20 made **one** denarius ($20 ÷ 20)

Talent

Worth 6,000 denarii*
(6,000 x $20)

Stater

Worth 3 denarii
(3 x $20.)

Drachm

Equal to a denarius

Kodrantes

About 80 made 1 denarius ($20 ÷ 80)

Lepton

About 160 made one denarius ($20 ÷ 160)

*Denarii is the plural form of denarius.

Jesus and His Family

Even though you don't hear a lot about them, Jesus did have half brothers and half sisters. They had the same mother, but not the same father. Their father was Joseph. Jesus' father was God. Mark 6:3 tells the names of His brothers: James, Joseph, Judas, and Simon. *Fill in the blanks with the correct member of Jesus' family.*

1. _____

His mother's husband, a carpenter (Matthew 1:24)

2._____

His mother (Matthew 1:24)

3. _____

Mary's first child (Luke 2:21-23)

4. _____

A half brother who became a disciple and perhaps wrote the 20th book in the New Testament (Mark 6:3)

5. _____

A half brother who may have written the Book of Jude (Mark 6:3)

6. _____

Another half brother (Mark 6:3)

7. _____

Another half brother (Mark 6:3)

8. Half sister. We don't know her name.

9. Half sister. We don't know her name.

Jesus' Family Members

Color and cut out the puppets on this page and tape each puppet to a spoon handle or Popsicle stick so that the handle or stick is at the head of the puppet. (See illustration.) You can make a house in which to play with the puppets. See pages 22 and 23 for directions.

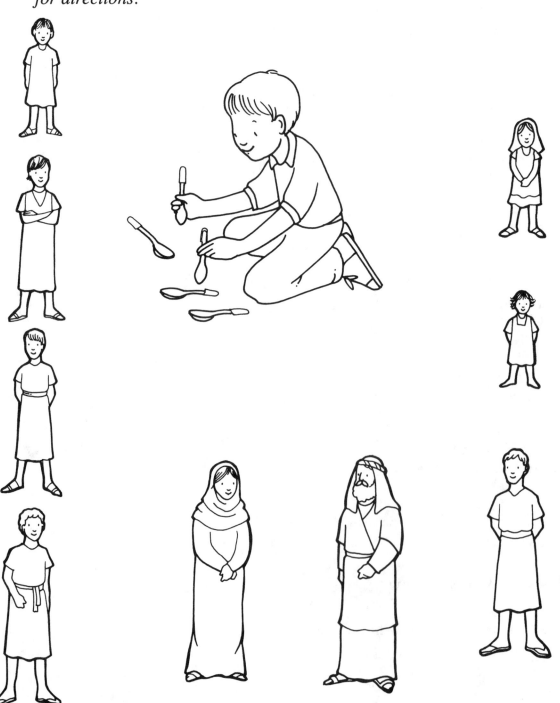

The Family of God

Jesus' family doesn't just include the people shown as puppets in this book. Everyone who accepts and follows Jesus is born again into the family of God. *Complete this short puzzle to find out about God's family.*

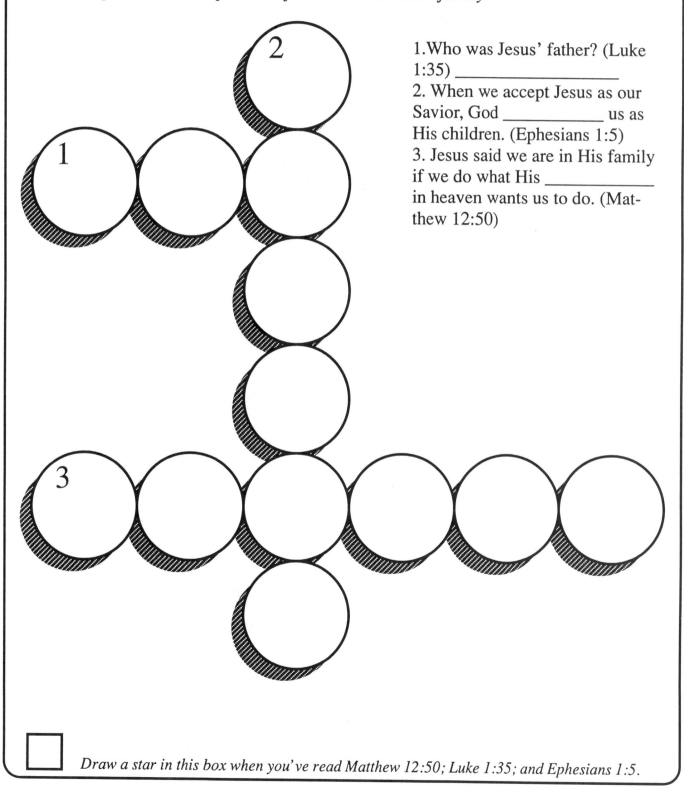

1. Who was Jesus' father? (Luke 1:35) _____

2. When we accept Jesus as our Savior, God _____ us as His children. (Ephesians 1:5)

3. Jesus said we are in His family if we do what His _____ in heaven wants us to do. (Matthew 12:50)

Draw a star in this box when you've read Matthew 12:50; Luke 1:35; and Ephesians 1:5.

Becoming Part of God's Family

Have you asked Jesus to save you from your sins and trusted Him as the only way you can live with God in heaven forever? If you have, then you're a member of God's family along with everyone else who trusts and follows Jesus! If you have questions about becoming a part of God's family, ask the person who gave you this page or book to explain more about accepting Jesus as your Lord and Savior.

The Family of God

These people have a good reason to be happy—they belong to God's family. However, there's one person who's missing and that's you. Finish drawing yourself to complete this picture of God's family.

House Matchups

Match things from your house with things from Jesus' house.

YOUR HOUSE

JESUS' HOUSE

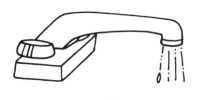

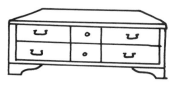

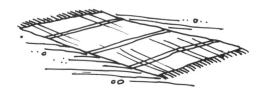

Make a Bible-Times House

Use the puppets from page 18 to act out what you think life may have been like in Jesus' home in Nazareth. Remember that Hebrews 4:15 tells us that Jesus never sinned.

The roof was probably made of branches with clay on top of them. It would have been very leaky. After a rain, people had to roll roofs out with a big roller to make them flat again. People spent a lot of time on the roof. Roofs had short walls or railings that kept people from falling off.

What You Need

- shoe box
- pudding box
- brown paper
- scissors
- tape
- markers
- glue
- potting soil
- colored cutouts from pages 23 and 24

What You Do

1. Cover the outside of the shoe box and the inside walls with brown paper and tape the paper in place. The houses in Jesus' day were usually made of clay bricks, so draw bricks with markers.

2. The houses in Jesus' day usually had dirt floors, so coat the bottom with glue and sprinkle potting soil on it.

3. Cut out holes for windows. Jesus' windows would not have had any glass in them.

4. Tape the pudding box shut and cover it with brown paper. Cut a piece of paper and fold it to look like stairs. Glue the box to the floor of the house and glue the "stairs" to the box and to the floor. This makes a platform where the family worked and slept. They usually kept animals inside the house on the lower floor.

5. The walls behind the platform had places carved out of them that stored sleeping mats and cooking utensils. The floor of the platform had a hole carved out of it for storing corn and other food; this was covered with a clay lid. The walls had troughs carved out of them that held animals' food. Cut these out from page 23 and glue them onto the walls and platform floor.

6. Cut out the other items from pages 23 and 24 and stand them inside the house or glue them onto the walls.

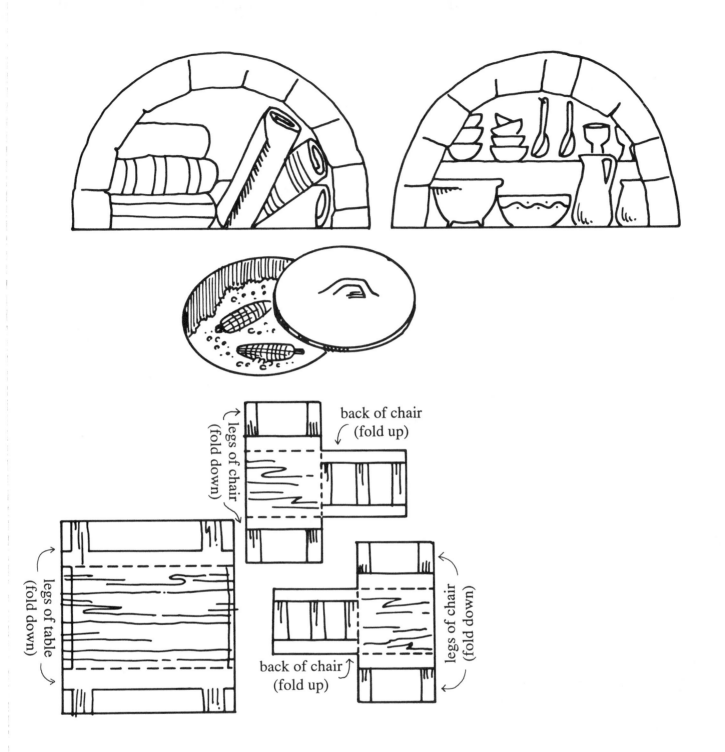

legs of chair
(fold down)

back of chair
(fold up)

legs of table
(fold down)

back of chair
(fold up)

legs of chair
(fold down)

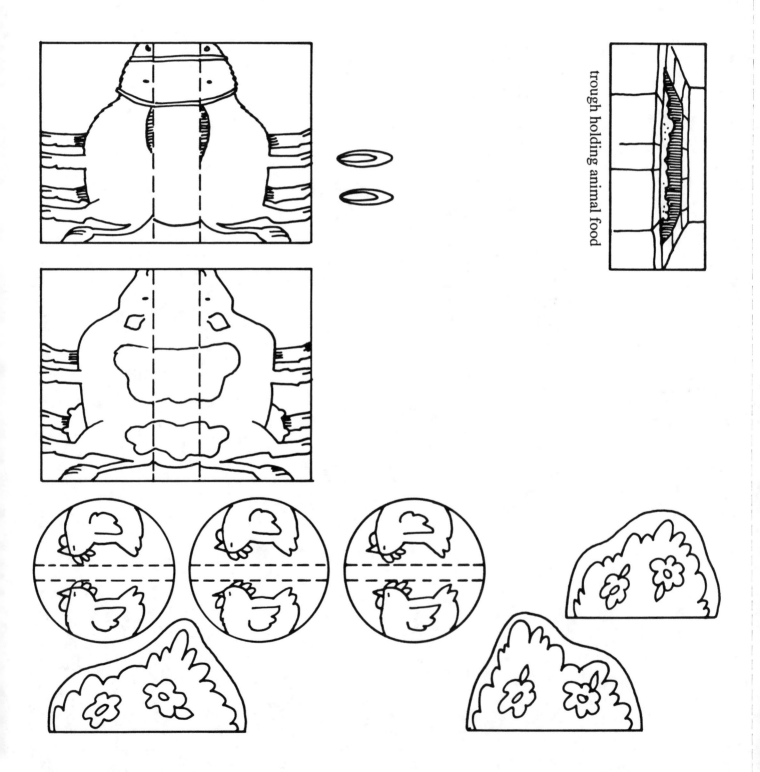

trough holding animal food

Woodworking with Joseph

Joseph was a carpenter. In Bible times, fathers usually trained their sons to do the same job they did, so Jesus probably learned woodworking. They may have made yokes (wooden bars that keep two animals joined while they are working together), wheels, troughs to hold animal food, and simple furniture.

Some people think Joseph may have died while Jesus was a teenager because Joseph isn't mentioned in the Bible after Jesus was twelve years old. If so, Jesus may have had to help earn a living for Mary and the rest of the family.

If you can, visit someone who does woodworking. As you watch him or her work, think about Jesus and Joseph. Think about how their tools would have been similar and different (remember that they didn't have electricity). Ask for some sawdust to take home for sawdust clay.

Sawdust Clay

What You Need
- 1 cup sawdust
- 1 cup flour
- 3/4 cup water

What You Do

1. Mix sawdust and flour together in a medium-size bowl.

2. Slowly add water, stirring until a dough forms. (You may not need all of the water.) If the clay is too dry, add a little more water. If it is too wet, add equal amounts of sawdust and flour.

3. After you have shaped the clay into an object, let it dry two or three days. Then you can sand it and paint it.

Play Bible-Times Games

In Jesus' day, Jewish children often played a game called "The Gap."

What You Need

• 12 pebbles

What You Do

Gently toss 12 pebbles upward. Flip your hand over and try to catch as many pebbles as you can on the back of your hand. Whoever catches the most pebbles wins.

'Jacob and Rachel'

Jewish children played this game that was based on an Old Testament story in which Jacob was tricked into marrying the wrong girl! He ended up with Leah when he wanted to marry Rachel.

What You Need

• 1 boy and at least 2 girls

What You Do

1. The boy stands in the middle of a circle of girls. The girls are holding out an arm to him.
2. He closes his eyes and the girls walk around him until he grabs a hand.
3. Without opening his eyes, he tries to guess whose hand he is holding.

If you are playing in a group that has more than one boy, boys should take turns being Jacob or there should be more than one circle of kids playing the game at the same time.

The Holidays Jesus Celebrated

The word *holiday* comes from the words *holy day*. In Old Testament times God told His people to celebrate special holy days each year. All Jewish males age twelve and older had to travel to Jerusalem for three feasts every year. They were 1) *Feast of the Passover and Unleavened Bread*, 2) the *Feast of Weeks or Pentecost*, and 3) the *Feast of Tabernacles*. What Jewish holidays are marked on your calendar?

THE DOOR OF MY

Color the door frame red like the blood of the Lamb if you have accepted Jesus as your Savior.

Passover (held in March or April)

To find out about Passover, first read the story and pass over every word that has a cross above it. When you reach the end, read the story a second time, reading only the words with the crosses above them.

The ✝anyone. Passover ✝Jesus was called when ✝Himself Jewish ✝the people Passover ✝remembered . ✝lamb. the ✝His night blood ✝God delivers ✝delivered ✝us them ✝from from ✝sin slavery and ✝in we ✝Egypt. ✝can The ✝trust people ✝Christ killed ✝to a forgive ✝lamb ✝us. and ✝He put died ✝its on ✝blood the on ✝cross ✝the for ✝doorposts. ✝us The ✝so angel ✝we passed can ✝over live ✝these forever ✝homes in and heaven didn't ✝someday. kill

The Holidays Jesus Celebrated
Feast of Unleavened Bread
(held immediately after Passover)

Cross the word leaven *out of each word to find out about this feast.*

Wleahevenn Gleaovd'sen pleeavopenle (Ilseavraeenlites) lweeavreen flreeeadven flreaovmen slleaavveenry leiavenn leEagvyepnt, lteahveeyn leleafvetn tloeaoven qleuiavckelny lteoaven pluetaven leavenleaven (wlehaavten mleaavkeesn lebavreenad rleaivseen leaanvend bleeavcoenme lleaigvhent) lineaven leatvheen leabvreenad ledavoughen. leaAvfteenr tlehaavetn, tlheeayven hleealvend letahveen lFeaeavsetn loeafven Unleavenleavened Brleaeavden leaeavcehn lyeaeavren.

Dleaurvening lteavheen fleaeavenst tlheeaveny leavenonly leaavteen flleaatven, unleavenleavened blreaeadven fleavenor aleaven weeleavenk leaanvend tlheaanvkeend Gloeavend fleavenor tleaakveinng thleeavmen leaouvetn olfeaven slealavvenery.

Most supermarkets sell unleavened bread you can buy to taste. It's called matzo.

28

The Holidays Jesus Celebrated

Feast of Weeks or Pentecost

(held 50 days after Passover)

This was a celebration of joy and it was a time when people thanked God for the blessings of a good wheat harvest. *Write or draw pictures of some of your blessings and thank God for them.*

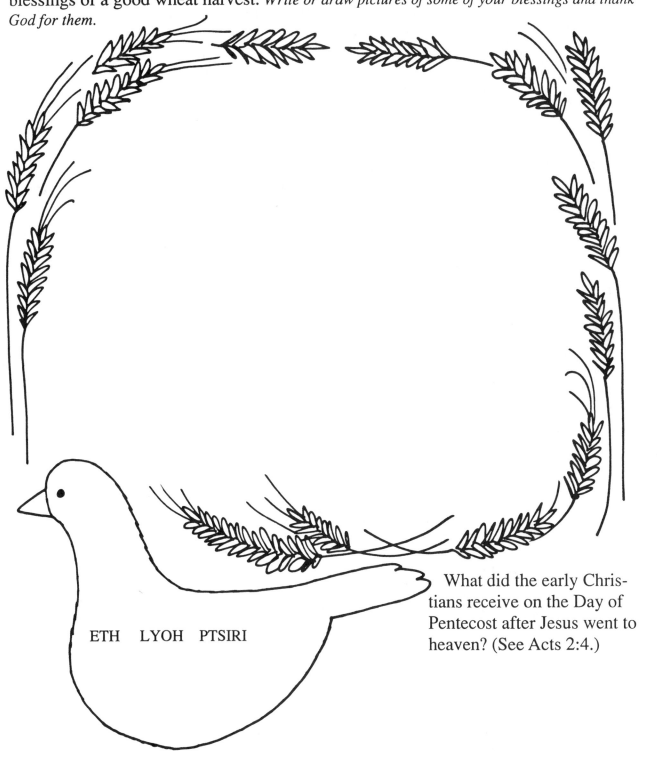

ETH   LYOH   PTSIRI

What did the early Christians receive on the Day of Pentecost after Jesus went to heaven? (See Acts 2:4.)

The Holidays Jesus Celebrated

The Feast of Tabernacles

(held in September or October)

The word tabernacle means *tent*. The Feast of Tabernacles was celebrated to remember that God's people lived in temporary shelters when God brought them out of Egypt. The feast was held when the fruit from the orchards had been harvested. People visiting Jerusalem, and even the people who lived in the city, camped in huts and tents like ones the children of Israel stayed in after they left Egypt.

Praise God in a tent like the Jews did during the Feast of Tabernacles.

Make a tent from chairs and a blanket. Take a picnic of fruit into the tent and thank God for blessing you with food to eat and for taking care of you like He took care of His people in the wilderness. Color the picture on this page.

Taste Foods Jesus Ate

When your parents are making up a grocery list, ask them to add a few of these foods that Jesus ate. Think about Jesus as you try some of the foods He ate.

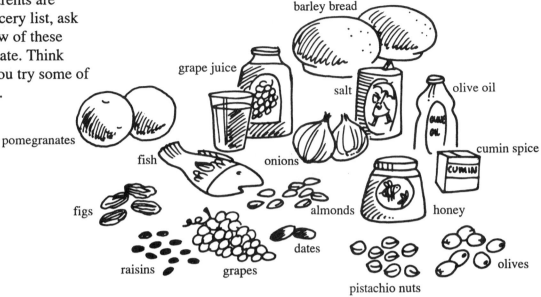

Make Grape Juice

Grapes were one of the main crops in the land where Jesus lived. Sometimes people used a press to crush grapes and drain the juice to make wine. Or they actually stepped on them with their bare feet! Try your hand—er, that is, your feet—at making some grape juice. Ask an adult to help you.

What You Need

- 1 pound of red seedless grapes
- newspaper
- gallon-size sealable plastic bag
- cardboard box
- paper towels
- large, sterile gauze bandages or cheesecloth

What You Do

1. Spread newspapers on the floor to protect it.
2. Wash the grapes and pull them off the stems. Then drop the grapes into the plastic bag. Squeeze the air out of the bag and seal it.
3. Lay the bag of grapes in a large cardboard box on top of the newspaper.
4. Take off your shoes and socks, and very carefully walk on the bag until the juice is mashed out of the grapes.
5. Hold a clean gauze bandage or piece of cheesecloth over a glass and carefully pour juice from the bag into the glass. When the glass is full, throw away the gauze and what it has strained out of the grape juice.
6. Enjoy your grape juice! Share it with your class or family.

School in Jesus' Day

Jewish places of worship were called synagogues (try to say that word ten times fast!) Each had a school attached to it. A Jewish boy began attending school at age five or six. Only boys went to school. There, the boys learned to read and study the Scriptures. Every child memorized the Shema, a group of Scriptures from the book of Deuteronomy.

For each blank, find the letter that has the same number and put it in that blank. Then memorize this verse (Deuteronomy 6:4, 5) that all Jewish boys, including Jesus, memorized.

A=17 B=25 C=19 D=12 E=49 F=71 G=3 H=15 I=4 J=1
K=39 L=20 M=7 N=14 O=2 P=5 Q=8 R=21 S=52 T=9
U=34 V=22 W=16 X=42 Y=26 Z=56

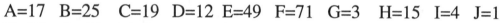

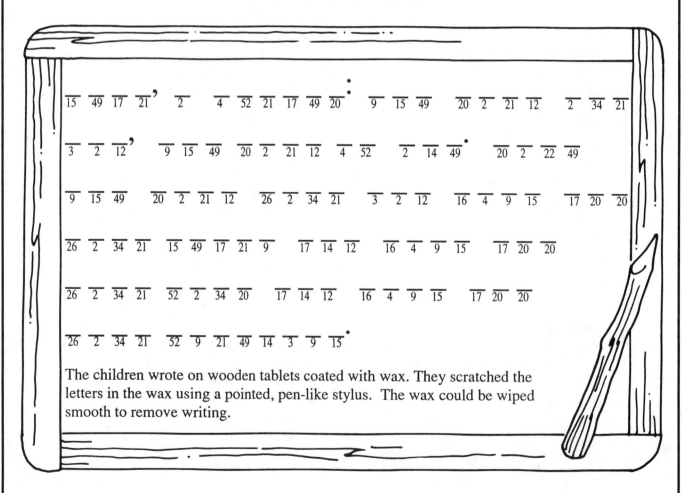

15 49 17 21 , 2   4 52 21 17 49 20 :   9 15 49   20 2 21 12   2 34 21

3 2 12 ,   9 15 49   20 2 21 12   4 52   2 14 49 .   20 2 22 49

9 15 49   20 2 21 12   26 2 34 21   3 2 12   16 4 9 15   17 20 20

26 2 34 21   15 49 17 21 9   17 14 12   16 4 9 15   17 20 20

26 2 34 21   52 2 34 20   17 14 12   16 4 9 15   17 20 20

26 2 34 21   52 9 21 49 14 3 9 15 .

The children wrote on wooden tablets coated with wax. They scratched the letters in the wax using a pointed, pen-like stylus. The wax could be wiped smooth to remove writing.

Where Jesus Worshiped

Find the underlined words in the puzzle. The words can be forward, backward, vertical, horizontal, or diagonal.

Jesus worshiped at a <u>synagogue</u>. The Jewish people met on <u>Saturdays</u> for <u>worship</u>. Saturday was their <u>sabbath</u>. Later Christians began to worship on <u>Sunday</u> because that was the day <u>Jesus</u> rose from the dead.

In the synagogue service, people recited <u>Scriptures</u> they had <u>memorized</u>, <u>listened</u> to other Scriptures being read, <u>talked</u> about what the scriptures meant, <u>prayed</u>, and <u>sang</u> <u>hymns</u> and <u>psalms.</u> The Scriptures and psalms they used were from the <u>Old Testament</u> of the Christian <u>Bible</u>.

```
R  D  S  M  L  A  S  P  J  T
H  Y  M  N  S  R  Y  D  W  N
L  P  S  A  N  G  N  B  O  E
B  L  D  O  P  D  A  S  R  M
E  I  N  M  R  E  G  A  S  A
R  S  B  F  A  Z  O  B  H  T
J  T  A  L  Y  I  G  B  I  S
D  E  R  D  E  R  U  A  P  E
E  N  S  Y  D  O  E  T  B  T
K  E  E  U  R  M  I  H  S  D
L  D  Z  R  S  E  U  K  A  L
A  O  V  W  R  M  L  E  F  O
T  S  Y  A  D  R  U  T  A  S
S  C  R  I  P  T  U  R  E  S
R  P  E  Y  A  D  N  U  S  K
```

Somebody and Something's Missing

Even though Mary knew that Jesus was God's Son, she and Joseph didn't understand all that it meant. After all, Jesus was their son to look after and care for as He grew. *Fill in the missing vowels to read a story about when Jesus was missing.* Vowels are **A, E, I, O,** and **U**.

_ v_ry y_ _r M_ry _nd J_s_ph w_nt t_
                    1   **2**
J_r_s_l_m f_r th_ F_ _st _f th_ P_ss_v_r. Wh_n
        3
J_s_s w_s tw_lv_, H_ w_nt w_th H_s f_m_ly t_
    4   **5**   **44**
J_r_s_l_m.

Wh_n th_y w_r_ r_t_rn_ng t_ N_z_r_th, M_ry
                                    56
_nd J_s_ph th_ _ght J_s_s w_s w_th _th_r
  6   **7**
p_ _pl_ _n th_ _r gr_ _p. Th_y tr_v_l_d f_r _
                                                8
d_y _nd th_n b_g_n _sk_ng f_m_ly _nd _th_rs
57   **9**   **10**
_f th_y kn_w wh_r_ J_s_s w_s. M_ry _nd J_s_ph
  11   **12**   **13**
c_ _ldn't f_nd J_s_s, s_ th_y w_nt b_ck t_
            14   **15**
J_r_s_l_m t_ l_ _k f_r H_m.
        16

_ft_r thr_ _ d_ys th_y f_ _nd J_s_s _n th_
                              17   **18**
t_mpl_ w_th t_ _ch_rs _ll _r_ _nd H_m. H_ w_s
        19   **20**   **21**   **22** **23 24 25**
l_st_n_ng t_ th_m _nd _sk_ng q_ _st_ _ns.
          26
_v_ry_n_ wh_ h_ _rd H_m w_s _m_z_d by H_s
  27 28   **29**

_nd_rst_nd_ng _nd _nsw_rs.
 30   31   55

M_ry s_ _d, "S_n, why h_ve Y_ _ tr_ _t_d _s
           32

l_k_ th_s? Y_ _ r f_th_r _nd _ h_ve b_ _n
33   34   35

s_ _rch_ng f_r Y_ _ _nd h_ve b_ _n v_ry _ps_t."
   36   37   38   39

J_s_s s_ _d, "Why w_r_ y_ _ s_ _rch_ng f_r
          40   41 42 43

M_? D_dn't y_ _ w_nt M_ t_ b_ d_ _ng My
45

F_th_r's w_rk?"
    46

_t th_ t_m_, M_ry _nd J_s_ph d_dn't _nd_rst_nd
          47   48

th_t J_s_s w_s t_lk_ng _b_ _t G_d th_ F_th_r.
                                      49

B_t M_ry r_m_mb_r_d wh_t J_s_s h_d s_ _d.
  51   50   54   52   53

Fill in the blanks to find something this story teaches.

1	2	3	4	5		6	7	8	9	10	11		12	13	14	15
16	17	18	19	20		21	22	23	24	25		26	27	28	29	30
31	32		33	34	35	36	37		38	39	40		41	42	43	44	45
46	47	48		49	50	51	52	53	54	,		55	56	57	.

Growing Like Jesus

Luke 2:40 says Jesus "grew and became strong; he was filled with wisdom, and the grace of God was upon him." Make a growth chart to see how you're growing. Each time you measure your height, ask yourself, "Have I grown to be a little more like Jesus?"

A Growth Chart to Make

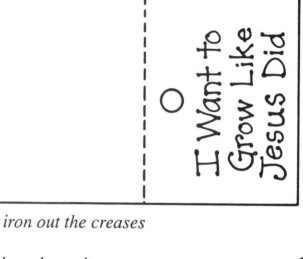

What You Need

- 6 feet of 1-inch wide bias tape
- measuring tape
- permanent markers
- scissors
- stapler
- paper hole punch
- adhesive tape

What You Do

1. Ask a grown-up to help you iron out the creases in the bias tape.

2. Using a measuring tape and markers, draw small lines one inch apart along an edge of the bias tape.

3. Start at what will be the bottom of the growth chart and count up to the twelfth mark. Write a large numeral 1 beside this mark. Count 12 marks from here and write a numeral 2. Count 12 marks from the numeral 2 and write a numeral 3. Count 12 marks from this mark and write a numeral 4, etc.

4. Cut out the growth chart holder and fold it in half. Color it and punch out the hole.

5. Place the top of the bias tape inside the holder and staple it.

6. Hang the growth chart so the bottom of it barely touches the floor. Tape the bottom of the chart to the wall.

7. Measure your height by standing the next to the chart.

Draw a star in this box when you've read Luke 2:40.

Jesus Obeyed His Parents

Luke 2:51 says that Jesus was obedient to His parents. Are you?

Underneath each of these faces, write something that your mom or dad told you to do today or yesterday. If you obeyed without complaining the first time your parent asked, draw a smile on the face. If you complained, had to be asked more than once, or disobeyed, draw a frown. Three smiles in a row make you a winner. Frowns don't win no matter how many are in a row.

Draw a star in this box when you've read Luke 2:51.

Grow Four Ways Jesus Grew

Luke 2:52 says "Jesus grew in wisdom and stature, and in favor with God and men." You can grow in these ways, too. *Look at the four ways Jesus grew and try to complete the goals for each way. As you complete each goal, color the goal's picture.*

1. In Wisdom (His mind grew)

For a whole day, think before you speak.

Before going to sleep, think about what you did during the day. What did you do well? Were there some things you could have done better? Ask God to help you with these things.

Read the Bible each day for a week.

2. In Stature (His body grew)

Cut out junk food for a day, and eat only healthy snacks.

Get to bed on time every day for a week.

Get some exercise every day for a week.

3. In Favor with God (His spirit grew)

Accept Jesus as your Savior. (Trust Him to make you able to go to heaven.)

Pray every morning and evening for a week.

Learn a new song, and then sing it as a praise to God.

4. In Favor with People (His personality grew)

Make a new friend.

Say only nice things for a day.

For a day, put yourself in everyone else's shoes. Each time you talk to someone, try to understand why he acts and feels the way he does.

What Would Jesus Do?

Jesus was once young like you. He understands what you're going through, because He became a person and lived on earth. When you're in difficult situations, ask Jesus to help you do what He would do in your situation. *For each of these situations, circle the answer that would help you become more like Jesus. When you're done, put the **letters** of the answers you circled in the blanks at the bottom of page 41 to find out how Jesus wants you to treat others.*

1. Someone unpopular wants to eat lunch with you.

B. Be nice, but eat as fast as you can.
L. Try to become friends and maybe introduce her to others.
J. Tell her you already promised to eat with someone else (even though you didn't).

2. One of your friends is thinking of taking drugs.

A. Say, "That may be okay for you, but I won't do it."
O. Ask an adult to explain why taking drugs is bad. Then explain it to your friend.
K. Don't say anything.

3. A friend says she's ashamed of something she did wrong.

D. Act shocked and say, "I would never do something like that!"
E. Say you won't play with someone like that.
V. Tell her God loves us and will forgive us when we do wrong things if we ask Him and put faith in Jesus.

4. Your brother has been yelling and slamming doors.

B. Tell your parents they ought to punish him.
E. Try to figure out what's bothering him and fix him a snack while you're fixing one for yourself.
H. Tell him to stop because he's putting you in a bad mood.

5. Someone copies your test and tells the teacher you copied her.

M. Tell everyone she's a cheater and to watch out for her.
O. Tell her you don't like her, and figure out how to get revenge.
T. Tell her how that made you feel and then forgive her.

6. A friend says she hopes she can do enough good things to get to heaven.

H. Tell her that we could never do enough good things to get to heaven. Encourage her to come to accept Jesus as Savior and follow Him.
N. Say, "You're such a nice person I'm sure you'll go there."
D. Don't say anything.

7. One of the kids at church doesn't come very often. How do you treat him?

J. Be glad you're a better person and don't say anything to him.
R. Tease him so he'll feel bad about not coming and will come more often.
E. Help him figure out why he doesn't come more and encourage him.

8. There's a new kid at school. What do you do?

K. Wait to see who makes friends with him before becoming his friend.
M. Introduce yourself and try to make him feel comfortable.
D. You already have enough friends, so don't say anything.

When you want to treat people as Jesus
would, all you have to remember is to . . .

____ ____ ____ ____   ____ ____ ____ ____
 1   2   3   4   5   6   7   8

I DID IT!

COMPLETED	DATE	COMPLETED	DATE
☐ Palestine, Where Jesus Grew Up	_____	☐ House Matchup	_____
☐ What's That?	_____	☐ Make a Bible-Times House	_____
☐ When Was Jesus Born?	_____	☐ Woodworking with Joseph	_____
☐ What a Little Bird Tells Us About Joseph and Mary	_____	☐ Play Bible-Times Games	_____
☐ Find Out What Simeon Said	_____	☐ The Holidays Jesus Celebrated	_____
☐ Jesus Escapes to Egypt	_____	☐ Taste Foods Jesus Ate	_____
☐ Make a Pyramid	_____	☐ Schools in Jesus' Day	_____
☐ What Jesus Probably Wore	_____	☐ Where Jesus Worshiped	_____
☐ The Languages Jesus Spoke	_____	☐ Somebody and Something's Missing	_____
☐ The Fish of Faith	_____	☐ Growing Like Jesus	_____
☐ Money in Bible Times	_____	☐ Jesus Obeyed His Parents	_____
☐ Jesus and His Family	_____	☐ Grow Four Ways Jesus Grew	_____
☐ The Family of God	_____	☐ What Would Jesus Do?	_____
☐ Becoming a Part of God's Family	_____		

ANSWERS

Page 5 1. Bethlehem; 2. Egypt; 3. Nazareth; 4. Jerusalem

Page 6 Swaddling - Clothes for wrapping a baby; Manger - Place where animal feed was kept; Stable - Place where animals were kept; Inn - Place for people to stay when they traveled; Tax - Money that was paid to the leaders of the country

Page 7 1. 4 B.C.
2. 6 B.C.
3. Answers will vary depending on year of using book

Page 9 The Holy Spirit had told a man named Simeon that he would not die until he saw the person who would save the world. When he saw the baby Jesus, Simeon said, "Now, I can die in peace." He knew Jesus was the one who would save the world. A woman named Anna knew it, too. Do you know it?

Page 10 An angel appeared to Joseph in a dream and told him to take Mary and Jesus to Egypt and to stay there until the angel told him to bring them back. The angel said the cruel king would try to kill Jesus. Joseph obeyed.
   Herod was probably afraid that Jesus would grow up and take his place on the throne. After King Herod died, Joseph, Mary, and Jesus moved to Nazareth in Galilee.

Page 13 1. Tunic; 2. Girdle; 3. Sandals; 4. Cloak; 5. Waistcloth

Page 14 1. Hallelujah; 2. Amen

Page 16 Talent - $120,000.00; Aureus - $500.00; Stater - $60.00; Didrachmon - $30.00; Drachm - $20.00; Assarion - $1.00; Kodrantes - 25¢; Lepton - 12 1/2¢

Page 17 1. Joseph; 2. Mary; 3. Jesus; 4. James; 5. Jude; 6. Joseph; 7. Simon

Page 19 1. God; 2. adopts; 3. Father

Page 27 The Passover was when Jewish people remembered the night God delivered them from slavery in Egypt. The people killed a lamb and put its blood on the doorposts. The angel passed over these homes and didn't kill anyone. Jesus called Himself the Passover lamb. His blood delivers us from sin and we can trust Christ to forgive us. He died on the cross for us so we can live forever in heaven someday.

Page 28 When God's people (Israelites) were freed from slavery in Egypt, they left too quickly to put leaven (what makes bread rise and become light) in the bread dough. After that, they had the Feast of Unleaven Bread each year.
   During the feast they only ate flat, unleavened bread for a week and thanked God for taking them out of slavery.

ANSWERS

Page 29   The Holy Spirit

Page 32   Hear, O Israel: The Lord our God, the Lord is one. Love the Lord your God with all your heart and with all your soul and with all your strength.

Page 33

```
R  D  S  M  L  A  S  P  I  T
H  Y  M  N  S  R  Y  D  W  N
L  P  S  A  N  G  N  B  O  E
B  L  D  O  P  D  A  S  R  M
E  I  N  M  R  E  G  A  S  A
R  S  B  F  A  Z  O  B  H  T
J  T  A  L  Y  I  G  B  I  S
D  E  R  D  E  R  U  A  P  E
E  N  S  Y  D  O  E  T  B  T
K  E  E  U  R  M  I  H  S  D
L  D  Z  W  R  E  U  K  A  L
A  O  V  W  R  M  L  E  A  O
T  S  Y  A  D  R  U  T  A  S
S  C  R  I  P  T  U  R  E  S
R  P  E  Y  A  D  N  U  S  K
```

Page 35   Jesus did not wait until He was grown to learn and serve His Father, God.

Page 41   Love them.

Index of *The Life and Lessons of Jesus* Series

BOOKS

1. Jesus Is Born
2. Jesus Grows Up
3. Jesus Prepares to Serve
4. Jesus Works Miracles
5. Jesus Heals
6. Learning to Love Like Jesus
7. Jesus Teaches Me to Pray
8. Following Jesus
9. Jesus Shows God's Love
10. Names of Jesus
11. Jesus' Last Week
12. Jesus Is Alive!

BIBLE STORY	LIFE AND LESSONS	BIBLE STORY	LIFE AND LESSONS
1st Miraculous Catch of Fish	Book 4	Great Commission	Book 12
2nd Miraculous Catch of Fish	Books 4, 12	Greatest Commandments	Books 6, 8
10 Disciples See Jesus	Book 12	Greatest Is Servant	Book 6
Angels Visit Shepherds	Book 1	Hairs Are Numbered	Book 9
As Father Has Loved Me . . .	Books 9, 11	Hand on Plow	Book 8
Ascension	Book 12	Healing at the Pool of Bethesda	Book 5
Ask in Jesus' Name	Book 11	Healing of 10 Lepers	Book 5
Ask, Seek, Knock	Book 7	Healing of a Blind Man	Book 6
		Healing of a Deaf and Mute Man	Book 6
Baby Jesus at the Temple	Book 2	Healing of a Leper	Book 5
Baptism of Jesus	Book 3	Healing of a Man's Hand	Book 5
Beatitudes	Books 6, 9	Healing of Blind Bartimaeus	Book 5
Becoming Child of God	Book 9	Healing of Centurion's Servant	Book 5
Belief and Baptism	Books 8, 12	Healing of Epileptic Boy	Book 5
Blind Leading Blind	Book 8	Healing of Malchus's Ear	Book 5
Boy Jesus at the Temple	Books 2, 3	Healing of Man Born Blind	Book 6
		Healing of Man with Dropsy	Book 5
Calming the Storm	Book 4	Healing of Official's Son	Book 5
Careless Words	Book 6	Healing of Peter's Mother-in-Law	Book 5
Christian Christmas Ideas	Book 1	Healing of the Paralytic	Book 5
Christian Easter Story and Activities	Books 11, 12	Healing of the Woman's Back	Book 5
Coin in Fish's Mouth	Book 4	Healing of Woman Who Touched Hem	Book 5
Count the Cost	Book 8	Heaven	Book 12
		How Much God Loves Us	Book 9
Demons into Pigs	Book 5	Humble Prayer	Book 7
Disciples Find a Donkey	Book 11		
Divorce/Stay Married	Book 6	I Am with You Always	Book 12
Do Not Let Your Heart Be Troubled	Book 11	I Live/You Will Live	Book 11
Don't Insult Others	Book 6	Include Others	Book 6
Don't Worry About Food and Clothes	Books 7, 9		
		Jesus Clears the Temple	Book 11
Endure to the End	Book 8	Jesus Died for Me	Book 9
Escape to Egypt	Book 2	Jesus Eats with Sinners	Book 9
Extra Mile	Book 6	Jesus Has Overcome the World	Book 11
		Jesus Is 'I AM'	Book 10
Faith of a Mustard Seed	Book 7	Jesus Is Arrested	Book 11
Faith to Move a Mountain	Book 7	Jesus Is Born	Books 1, 2
Fasting	Book 7	Jesus Is Buried	Book 11
Feed My Sheep	Book 12	Jesus Is Christ	Books 3, 10
Feeding the 5,000 and 4,000	Book 4	Jesus Is Crucified and Dies	Book 11
Forgive	Books 6, 7	Jesus Is God	Book 10
Forgiven Much, Love Much	Book 9	Jesus Is Immanuel	Book 10
		Jesus Is Tempted	Book 3
Gabriel Visits Mary	Book 1	Jesus Is the Bread of Life	Book 10
Garden of Gethsemane	Book 11	Jesus Is the Bridegroom	Book 10
Get Rid of What Causes Sin	Book 8	Jesus Is the Chief Cornerstone	Book 10
Gift of Holy Spirit	Books 9, 12	Jesus Is the Gate	Book 10
Give and Lend	Book 6	Jesus Is the Gift of God	Book 10
Give to Caesar What Is Caesar's	Book 8	Jesus Is the Good Shepherd	Book 10
God and Money	Book 8	Jesus Is the Lamb of God	Book 10
God Gives Good Gifts	Book 7	Jesus Is the Light	Book 10
God Wants Us in Heaven	Book 9	Jesus Is the Redeemer	Book 10
Golden Rule	Book 6	Jesus Is the Resurrection and Life	Book 10
Good Deeds in Secret	Book 8	Jesus Is the Savior	Book 10

Index of *The Life and Lessons of Jesus* Series

*If you would like to write the author,
send your letter to:*

Your address here

Stamp

Tracy L. Harrast
c/o Church Resources Dept.
David C. Cook Publishing Co.
850 N. Grove Avenue
Elgin, IL 60120